www.FlowerpotPress.com
CHC-1010-0595
Made in China/Fabriqué en Chine

BEES

Honeybees, Bumblebees, and More!

Written by **Dr. Shirley Raines**

Photography by **Curt Hart**

Discover bees with photos, fun facts, and verse

Integrating science and art creates a valuable and unique learning experience that particularly benefits the youngest of readers. STEAM (science, technology, engineering, art, and mathematics) education inspires a wider audience to invest in studying subjects from multiple perspectives and promotes an education that suits many types of learners.

In this introduction to bees, artistic and scientific elements are combined to create a comprehensive learning experience for young readers.

Continue the learning with a selection of engaging exercises in the back of the book. These Story S-t-r-e-t-c-h-e-r-s by Dr. Shirley Raines expand the material with a variety of activities perfect for learning both in and out of the classroom.

A glossary can also be found in the back of the book with words and definitions that help build upon the vocabulary from both the poetry and facts.

What's All the Buzz About?

Bumblebees and honeybees are like cousins. They are alike in some ways but also different.

They both make honey, but honeybees make much more honey than bumblebees.

Bumblebees are larger, rounder, and hairier than honeybees.

Bumblebees live in smaller colonies. Sometimes they build their hives underground. Honeybees live in very large colonies and build their hives above ground.

There are over 225 species of bumblebees around the world!

Bumblebees can use their stingers more than once. Honeybees can only use theirs once.

Female bumblebees, just like female honeybees, are the only ones that have a stinger.

Bumblebees flap their wings back and forth, rather than up and down.

Hot Body Bees

· ·

When the sun is boiling down,
in the pool is where I'm found.

Getting hot in the summer sun.
Don't let sweat bees ruin the fun!

All they want is a little salt.
So really it's not their fault.

Stay calm and try not to cry.
Just let that sweat bee fly on by.

Now you're dried off so it's back to the pool,
perfect for staying nice and cool.

And that little sweat bee is flying away
in search of flowers on this hot day!

No Sweat!

The reason sweat bees are attracted to sweat is pretty simple. They just want some moisture and salts.
If you feel a sweat bee on you, don't panic. Sweat bees are unlikely to sting unless provoked. Instead, just
gently brush the insect off or wait for them to leave. Make sure you don't hurt them. Sweat bees pollinate
flowers just like other bee species so they are very important.

Sweat bees can be many different colors, such as blue, purple, or green.

Most sweat bees make their hives underground out of dirt.

Sweat bee stings are among the least painful stings a person can feel.

More Holes

· ·

Making holes is lots of fun!
One hole here. It's just begun.

Boring holes with no tools.
Powerful jaws chew, chew, chew.

A hole in the post on our patio.
Where does this little hole go?

What's making holes
like little wood bowls?

Spilling tiny sawdust all around.
Carpenter bees make a sawing sound.

What "Wood" a Carpenter Bee Do?

Carpenter bees are best known for carving tunnels in wood. That is where they lay eggs. Since carpenter bees prefer to live alone, there is usually only one bee living in a tunnel. Tunnels can be found in trees or even wooden furniture or houses.

Carpenter bees are often confused with bumblebees. You can tell them apart because carpenter bees have a shiny abdomen and bumblebees have a furry abdomen.

Carpenter bees hibernate in the winter.

Carpenter bees live on every continent but Antarctica.

Queen Bee Questions

. . . .

Is the queen bee sitting on a throne?
Where is the queen bee's home?

Does she wear a crown?
Or a fancy ball gown?

Is she the one who eats royal jelly?
Does she have a very large belly?

Is the queen bee really large?
Is the queen bee the one in charge?

Does she have a big family?
Like me, does she live happily?

It's Hard Work Being Queen

The life of a queen bee starts when she is laid by the current queen. Many eggs are laid, but only one will become queen. All the larvae feed on royal jelly, however, only the future queen continues to eat royal jelly. From a larva, the queen develops into a pupa and after about 15 days, she chews her way out of the wax shell she is in. The new queen then takes the throne and begins her duties. Although her name makes her sound like royalty, she acts more like a mother of the hive rather than a ruler.

Queen honeybees can live up to 5 years!

A queen can lay up to 2,000 eggs per day.

The queen bee is the largest bee in the hive.

Queens, Workers, Drones, Oh My!

· ·

Bees live together in a colony or hive. The largest bee in the colony is called the queen. She lays the eggs.

Worker bees are small females that collect pollen and nectar. They take care of the hive and the queen.

Drones are male bees that mate with the queen.

When a hive gets too crowded, bees will swarm. The old queen takes worker bees with her to create a new hive. A new queen takes over the old hive.

Most of the bees in a colony are worker bees.

A honeybee colony can consist of up to 60,000 bees in the warmer months of the year.

In warmer months, there are a few hundred drones living in the colony. When the weather gets colder, the workers kick the drones out of the hive.

Busy Honeybees

Honeybees, honeybees, buzzing around.
Honeybees, honeybees, flying up and down.

A hive is where you can find a honeybee.
They are usually hiding near a rock or a tree.

On a beautiful day, so bright and sunny,
these bees work hard to make their honey.

They leave the hive to find a bloom
and fill their pollen sacs 'til there's no room.

Then back to the hive with their prize in tow
to keep the hive strong and continue to grow.

The Power of Pollination

Nearly one third of the food we eat is a result of pollination. Pollination is an important process in a plant's life cycle and allows for more plants to be created. As honeybees collect the pollen and nectar they need for their hive, they also pollinate crops that humans eat along the way. The pollen sticks to the bee's fuzzy body and then falls off as the bee travels from plant to plant, allowing the plants to reproduce.

Honeybees pollinate more than 90 different crops across the United States.

Honeybees can beat their wings 200 times per second.

Bees help pollinate to create some of our favorite foods, including apples, avocados, blueberries, peaches, and so many more!

Counting the Anatomy of a Honeybee

Count the body parts and see
what a complex insect is the honeybee.

Honeybee Head
2 antennae for touch and smell.
2 compound and 3 single lens eyes.
1 proboscis; a tongue like a straw.
2 mandibles; very strong jaws.

Thorax
1 muscular midsection makes them strong.
2 large translucent forewings help them fly along.
2 hind wings twist up and down.
3 pairs of legs for a total of 6.
2 pollen baskets to carry pollen.
6 claws on each leg to help them climb.

Abdomen
1 queen's place to carry eggs.
4 pairs of wax glands. That's 8.
1 stinger to sting
just once.

HONEYBEE

Hard outer shell called an exoskeleton

Two compound eyes

Three main body parts:
Head
Thorax
Abdomen

Two pairs of wings

One pair of
antennae attached
to their head

Three pairs of legs

Pollinator, Gladiator

. . . .

Little insect gladiator.
Expert navigator.

Searching for the hive.
Pollen to keep the queen alive.

Nectar collector.
Pollinator.

Bloom to bloom.
Fly home soon.

Superb Symbiosis

The relationship between plants and bees is a form of symbiosis. This means that both parties benefit. The plants benefit by having their pollen spread to help with reproduction, and the bees benefit by obtaining pollen that they then can eat and use in the hive.

Since bees cannot see the color red, they are more attracted to flowers that are blue, purple, or yellow.

Pollen that is brought back to the hive is often combined with nectar or honey to produce a substance called bee bread.

Bees can visit thousands of different flowers per day!

Waggle Dance

· ·

What's the chance
you can do a waggle dance?

The dance is a movement that is true.
It is a dance that bees like to do.

Wiggling and waggling their bodies and wings
are signals pointing toward important things.

Which direction should they go?
That is what a waggle dance will show.

Fly this way or that, then turn over here;
coneflowers and daffodils are near.

Sip your nectar, then fly back home.
Then once again back out to roam.

Bee Boogie

If a worker bee finds a great source of food, such as a flower with plenty of nectar, she might perform what is called a waggle dance when she returns to the hive. The dance is a way for bees to communicate with one another. Bees are able to give directions and distances through specific movements. The dance looks almost like a bee is drawing a figure eight with its body.

Bees can let other bees know if a flower has so much nectar that it will require multiple bees to harvest.

Scientists are still learning how bees are able to interpret the movements of a waggle dance.

Experienced bees can adjust their waggle dance to the changing direction of the sun.

Hexagon Honeycomb Mystery

Why do bees build their honeycombs with cells in hexagon shapes? The hexagon shape holds the most amount of honey without using as much wax. A hexagon has equal sides that fit together when stacked or lined up.

Many bees can work together building in different areas at the same time. The shapes all fit together.

It takes about 6 to 8 pounds (2.7 to 3.6 kilograms) of honey to make 1 pound (0.5 kilograms) of wax.

Bees use their body temperature to control the temperature of the honeycomb.

A honeycomb is where the bees store honey, pollen, and eggs.

Honeycombs are built by the worker bees out of beeswax.

Beehive Woman, Beehive Man

. . . .

Wear a hat and mask
for an important task.

Cover me up in a funny suit?
Honey, honey is our loot.

Can you tell me, beehive woman, beehive man,
why does the smoke come from your can?

Smoke the bees to keep them calm.
Now they know you mean no harm.

Keeper of Bees

While
beekeeping can be an
enjoyable hobby, it can also serve
a very important role in bee preservation
and food production. Some beekeepers provide
pollination services to farmers and maintain
hives on farms so the bees can help pollinate crops.
Others use their hives to produce things like honey,
royal jelly, and pollen. There are even beekeepers who
only raise queen bees for other beekeepers.

Beekeepers use smoke to keep the bees calm when they are inspecting the hive.

The practice of beekeeping began about 4,500 years ago by the Egyptians.

Beekeepers go by a number of names including honey farmers, apiarists, and apiculturists.

Licky, Sticky Honey

I like honey, oh so sweet!
I like honey. It's fun to eat!

Eating honey from the jar;
sticky sweetness like a candy bar.

But who makes my delicious treat?
This honey maker I would love to meet!

Bees, of course, as you can see.
They love honey as much as me!

Hold On to Your Honey

Besides eating it, there have been and still are lots of different uses for honey. In Germany in the 11th century, it was so popular that it was used as a form of payment. It can also be used to heal cuts and burns because it naturally kills bacteria.

The flowers bees visit most can affect how the honey they make looks and tastes.

A single honeybee will produce about 1/12 of a teaspoon (0.4 milliliters) of honey in its lifetime.

If honey is stored in an air-tight container, it never expires.

Conservation of the Colonies

Here are some ways to help preserve bee colonies:

- Plant bee-friendly flowers, such as honeysuckle, coneflowers, or sunflowers, in your garden to help bees pollinate in your area.

- When you see a bee, let it be! Leaving bees alone is an easy and helpful way to keep bees safe.

- Put a small tray of water out for bees to drink from on a windowsill or patio.

- Go to your local farmer's market and buy homemade honey or beeswax.

- Consider taking classes about insects. The more you learn, the more you can help.

- Celebrate World Bee Day on May 20 of each year.

STORY S-T-R-E-T-C-H-E-R-S

Stretch out the learning with this collection of activities created specifically to enhance the material and provide new ways to discover the wonderful world of bees. From language arts to mathematics and science, each activity incorporates information from the book and provides a new approach to teaching early learners in and out of the classroom. For more Story S-t-r-e-t-c-h-e-r-s, please visit www.FlowerpotPress.com.

Story S-t-r-e-t-c-h-e-r for LANGUAGE ARTS

What the children will learn
To organize information about bees and seek answers to questions

Materials
White board, poster board, or chart tablets and markers or pencils

What to do
1. Prepare a K-W-L chart. The K column is for what we already know about bees. The W is what we want to know about bees. The L is for what we learn. The L comes at the end of this exercise.
2. With the whole class or in small group discussions, complete the K and W columns.
3. Read the book.
4. Reread the list of items in the K column for what we already knew about bees. For older children, ask them to change any fact that they listed in the K column that they found to be false after reading the book. They can restate the fact.
5. Review the W column and write the answers in the L column.
6. Add new facts the children learned that went beyond their questions to the L column. Discuss each column and compare them.

Something to think about
Have children complete individual K-W-L charts. Emphasize that some people already know a great deal about bees, while others are just beginning to learn about them. Give some examples of what you, as the teacher or librarian, learned from the book. If all the children's original questions are not answered in the book, seek help from some other sources.

Story S-t-r-e-t-c-h-e-r for SCIENCE AND MATHEMATICS

What the children will learn
To recall the major body parts of the bee and to add and multiply their body parts

Materials
White board, dry-erase markers, markers, poster board, small magnets, and scissors

What to do
1. Copy the "Counting the Anatomy of a Honeybee" shape poem.
2. Highlight the key words in red or a bright color. Head: antennae, eyes, proboscis, mandibles; thorax: midsection, wings, legs, pollen baskets, claws; abdomen: eggs, wax glands, stinger.
3. Discuss the functions of each of the body parts.
4. Write keywords on poster board. Tape small magnets to the white board and to the backs of the poster board words. Let the children place the keywords on the shape poem in the correct part of the anatomy.
5. For mathematics, have the children add up the number of body parts mentioned in the poem.

Something to think about
Educators often hesitate to use large

words with young children, but children enjoy knowing them. Because of the unique shape of the words, such as proboscis, they may learn those words quickly. This Story S-t-r-e-t-c-h-e-r can easily be adapted for simpler or more complex lessons by using more intricate or more simplified anatomy diagrams.

Story S-t-r-e-t-c-h-e-r for MOVEMENT

What the children will learn
To imitate a bee's waggle dance

Materials
Construction paper flowers and "Flight of the Bumblebee" recording or buzzing bee video online

What to do
1. Read the "Waggle Dance" poem. Discuss what it means as a group.
2. Demonstrate the waggle dance by flapping your arms as if they were wings and pointing in different directions.
3. Pair the children up and let them practice wiggling and waggling their bodies and their wings without making a sound.
4. Place the construction paper flowers around the room and have the children extend their arms for their bee wings and practice giving directions to their partner.
5. After the children have worked on their waggle dancing, play "Flight of the Bumblebee" and let them fly around and give directions to their partners.
6. Have the children join small groups with one leader performing waggle dances to help the others find flowers.

Something to think about
Consider involving the physical education teacher or music teacher in this activity if you are fortunate to have them in your school. For older children, ask them to seek more information on bees and their communication.

Story S-t-r-e-t-c-h-e-r for ART

What the children will learn
To make designs from hexagons

Materials
Poster board, scissors, pencils, construction paper, and glue

What to do
1. Read "Hexagon Honeycomb Mystery."
2. Cut the poster board into flat hexagon shapes with the scissors. If your children are old enough, feel free to let them join in on making hexagons.
3. Demonstrate how to hold the hexagon patterns and trace around them with a pencil to draw hexagons on the construction paper.
4. If old enough, encourage children to cut out three-dimensional hexagon designs from the construction paper or poster board. Then glue the sides together.

Something to think about
Children can also create a hexagon pattern from poster board and construct a hexagon building. Show pictures of houses with hexagon shaped roofs or interior designs.

GLOSSARY

Abdomen: the lowest part of a bee's body, below the thorax

Antennae: rod-shaped body parts found on a bee's head; used to smell and maintain balance

Bee Bread: the pollen or honey eaten by bees

Beeswax: wax created by bees that is used to make honeycombs

Colony: a group of bees that live together, typically in a hive

Compound Eye: a type of eye bees have which is made up of thousands of lenses

Conservation: preserving and protecting our environment as well as the animals and plants within it

Exoskeleton: the outer hard shell bees have to protect their bodies

Hive: the place where a collection of bees live, typically made from wood if created by a beekeeper

Honeycomb: wax shaped into hexagons where pollen, honey, and eggs are stored

Larva: the first stage of a bee's life

Mandibles: mouth organs near the front of a bee's mouth

Nectar: sweet secretion from flowers that bees eat and turn into honey

Pollen: the spores on a plant that bees carry for later use

Pollen Sac: a cavity on a bee where pollen is stored

Pollination: when pollen is introduced to a plant's stigma, starting the process for reproduction

Proboscis: a hollow tube on a bee's head used to drink liquid

Pupa: the stage of a bee's life after larva but before adult

Reproduction: when plants produce seeds to make new plants

Royal Jelly: a substance secreted by worker bees that is fed to bee larvae

Swarm: when the current queen bee leaves a crowded hive with worker bees to start a new hive somewhere else

Symbiosis: a relationship between two organisms in which both parties benefit from the relationship

Thorax: the middle part of a bee's body